My Story
Noah

My adventure on the ark!

Written by Fiona Boon.

Illustrated by Nadine Wickenden.

make
believe
ideas

My STORY

ME

Hello, my name is Noah. Let me **introduce** the **people** in my story.

I'll go first – I'm **six hundred** years old! I live with my **family** and we all try to **respect** God.

This is my loving wife. She's very patient with me.

MY WIFE

2

These are my **sons** – **Shem** is the oldest, then **Ham**, then **Japheth**.

JAPHETH

HAM

SHEM

HIGH ROOF

This is the **ark**. It is a **huge boat** made of cypress wood. All kinds of **animals** boarded the **ark** with us.

CYPRESS WOOD

3

I was **standing** in the **warm sunshine** one day when God came to me with some **crazy news**. He said, "I have had enough of people **hurting** each other and **disobeying** me. I am going to DESTROY everything on the **earth**. Noah, I want you to **build** a huge boat to keep you and your family **safe**."

ANGRY MAN

ARGH!

HAM

USEFUL TOOLS

I was **totally** confused. We live **nowhere** near

the **sea**, and it **hardly** RAINS here.

My **neighbours** would think I was mad! But I

did **not** want to **question** God, so I called my

sons together and we started to **build** the ark.

JAPHETH

God had also **said**: "FILL the **ark** with two of **every kind** of land animal and bird, and **take** every kind of food so that you do not go **hungry**."

FOOD STORES

SHEM

How was I going to get all the animals **together**? I had no idea, but as we **finished** building the **ark**, something strange happened.

MY VERY LONG LIST

9

STOMP!

TWEET!

HISS!

From **every direction**, animals began

to come towards the **ark**. There were enormous

elephants and slithering snakes, tiny birds

and tall giraffes. They came in **pairs**, a male

and a female together. And they **all** came **quietly**,

with no thought of **attacking** each other.

HUGE DOOR

Amazingly, ALL the animals fitted **comfortably** inside the HUGE ark.

Meanwhile, my wife and the boys **stowed away** every kind of food they could **find**.

Finally, the **whole family** climbed on board – feeling a bit silly.

Our **neighbours** gathered and LAUGHED at us.

But then the **rain** started . . .

RAIN

SACKS OF FOOD

13

GIANT WAVES

and **didn't stop!**

For FORTY days and **nights**, it rained, until the **earth** was **completely** flooded.

We **floated** on the waters for **weeks**, without seeing so much as the **tip** of a **mountain-top**.

Once the **rain** had **stopped**, we **waited** for the **waters** to go down. I sent out a **raven** and then a **dove** to **look** for **land**, but they **both** came back with NOTHING. A **week** later, I sent the **dove** out again. **This time** it brought back an **olive leaf**.

CALM SEA

OLIVE LEAF

17

A few days later, I sent the **dove** out once more.

This time, it didn't come back **at all**.

"**Good**!" I thought. "It has found **dry land**."

DRY LAND

18

The **ark** came to **rest** in some hills.

But it was many more days before God
FINALLY **told** us we could **leave** the ark.

19

ALTAR

BLEAT!

GOD'S RAINBOW

I built an **altar** to God to **thank** him for keeping us safe. In **return**, God **showed** us a wonderful **rainbow**, as a **promise** that he would **never** DESTROY the **earth** again.

21

My Sticker Journal

Can you remember my story?

Use the **stickers** to complete my journal.

God told me to build a **huge** boat to keep **me** and my family safe.

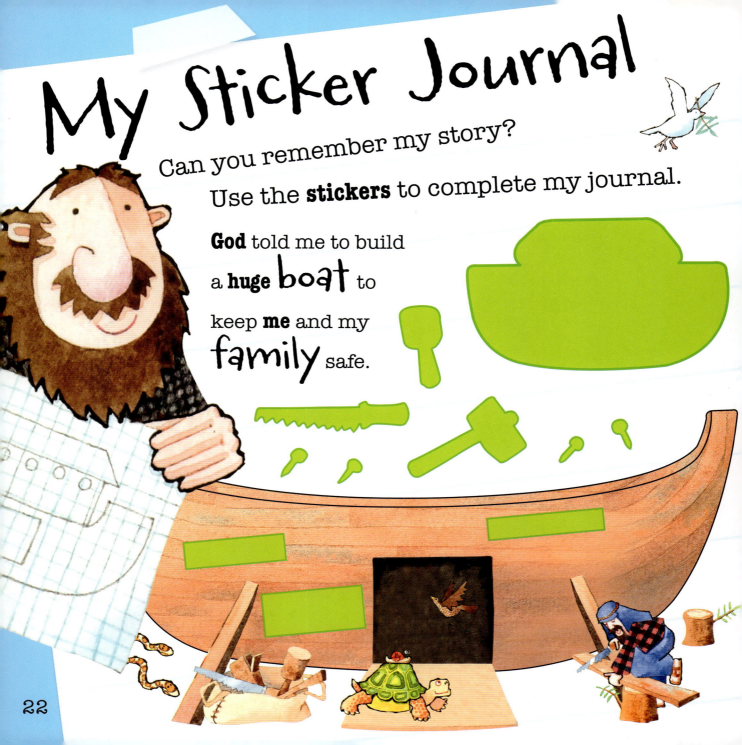

Then the **animals** came **two-by-two**.

Find two butterflies.

Colour a tall giraffe.

Animals eat a **lot** of food so I needed a **long list**.

Sticker the food and tick the box once you have found it.

The **animals**
filled the **ark**.

Draw your two favourite animals.

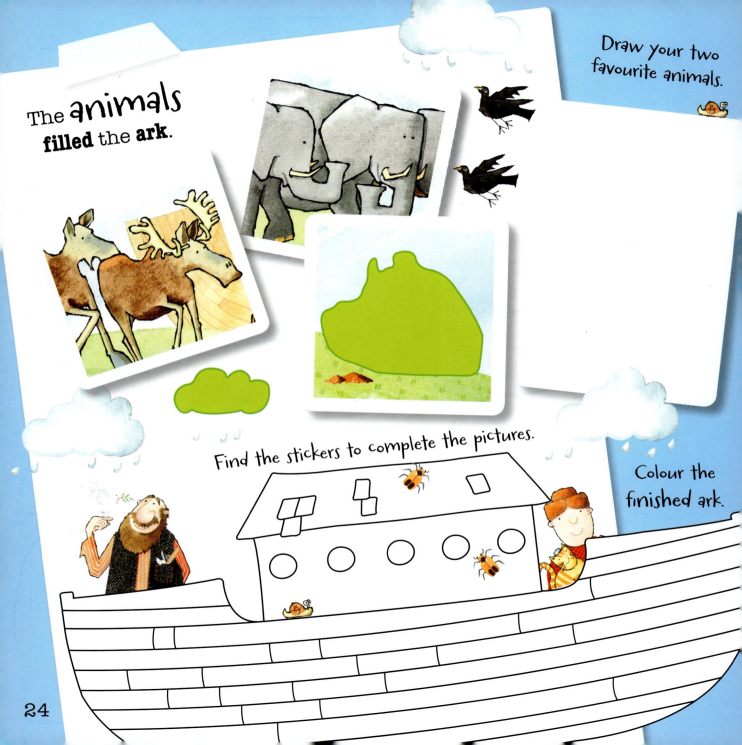

Find the stickers to complete the pictures.

Colour the finished ark.